Arias of Ecstasy

Devotional Poems Dedicated to my Guru

Adi Da Samraj

by Michele Krueger

copyright©2014 by Michele Krueger

ISBN-13: 978-1500334000

Cover Art by Patti Jahsmine

All Along

for years
I ran to Darshan
to catch a glimpse of Him,
to prostrate at His Feet
with fragrant offerings

but I did not renounce my life

I walked back home to be a wife
and write a rural fiction

I neglected Him

it was not until
my husband turned to ash
scattered on an ocean reef

that I Heard Him
Whisper in my ear
Louder than my grief
that He'd Been Waiting here
All Along

and He Chaperoned me
Home
to be His Own

Almost Erased

my stenciled self
is evaporating

being penciled out
of its limited perimeter

condensing into
His Bliss

Uncontained

and Spreading

Archer

His Arrows of Light
thrust deep into the dark of self

wedging between ribs
to Flicker a Flame
to Kindle a Glow

to diminish
ego

in all who have grown weary
of stumbling

His Feathered Darts

Fly Straight to the heart

Arias of Ecstasy

I am not
an opera singer
and yet,
arias of ecstasy
quiver on my lips

I do not know
positions of ballet
but still,
my body fills with Light,
and moves me as It will

in matters of the Heart
I was not trained,
but by the Rarest Grace

I've memorized His Name!

Arrival Mala

when the wide wooden doors
of All Eyes Gate opened

a conch shell would punctuate
the Potent Air
Announcing Him

devotees would catch their breath
in exultation

as He Emerged,
Silent, Fiery, Effulgent

to Do the Heart's Work here

to Step Foot
to Stand Firm

to Receive our gifts

a strand of pungent flowers
planted and plucked from my
garden
strung with His Holy Name
on my tongue

lifted over His Head

and come to
final fragrant rest

on the Great One's Chest

At Your Altar

let the sun rise
and drench the morning skies
with birdsong

let daffodils lift
their liquid gold
to gather sifted light

I only long to linger
at Your Altar

to rest my head
in a tuft of rug

to shrug off this shroud
and be nakedly Yours

eternally bowed

Boutonniere

when I could not take another
breath
You Gave me Mouth to Mouth

when my heart lost its beat
You Turned Up Your Jukebox
and Danced me

You Have Donned me
like an overcoat
out on a winter stroll

I've become a white carnation

inside Your Buttonhole

Branded By Your Love

when a devotee
who has been listening
begins to understand

there is a glisten on his skin
a glimmer in her eye
a sigh on his lip

a soul incision made
that will never fade

linked by devotion
inked by Grace
scrawled across our hearts
in a Font of Truth

a Tattoo of You

Chameleon

if I could change my form
I would be the towering palm
frond
to gently fan You

I would shade You
from the scorch of summer
with my tropical umbrella

I'd be the leather sandals
under Your Feet
and have You Rest Your Blissful
Weight
upon me

I would carry You
wherever Your Wandering
Demanded
and cradle Your Soles
with a calm devotion

I would be the balm
to heal Your Afflictions
the cloth to cool Your Forehead
the purest water to bathe
Your Human Form

I would spread myself before You
as a thousand fragrant marigolds

to line Your Holy Foot Path

**and when You'd Deign
to Stand and Grant Your Gifts
to ease our pain**

the ebony would gleam

as You Leaned against

my cane

Circle Dance

I have been climbing
His Spherical Staircase
up spirals of time

I have been orbiting around
An Effulgent Sun
for unknown eons

a lunar moth drawn
to His Flame-
wings flapping
a circumambulation

a puja candle waved
in pensive contemplation

a wrist stroke
a wisp of incense smoke
wafting in the air

all urged to trace
ecstatic rings
around His Murti Face

Clairol

years ago
I dyed my hair a lighter color
and no one noticed

not long after
while serving at the Ashram
I walked to the Bathhouse
for a quiet dip

I stripped
and entered the large plunge
foggy with moist air

and There
Laughing with His daughters
was the Guru
Standing in those Blessing waters

I sat stone still
a boulder of separation
sensing I'd intruded
and doubting
what I meant to Him

until He Tenderly
Swam up to me
Sat down Thigh to thigh
Knee to knee

to Point out His Polio Leg

then Leaned in to Whisper

softly in my ear

like I was the cherished one

you changed the shade

of your hair

Deluge

**at Darshan
a single Tear
rolled down His Cheek
Bursting with Bliss**

**it lingered at the tip
of His Chin**

until it Dripped

**a Deluge
to purify the universe**

in One Blessing Drop

Despite My Grasp

forms shift and dissolve
like sand sifting
through my fingers

rising ashes
buried bones

only
apparently alone

to swoon
in a Love
that never abandons

a Love
that hoists us
from the mire
of merely fulfilling
mortal desire

a Love
That Points the Way

to cleave our fragile hearts

to Only That Which Stays

A Soundless Deep

these words are not my own
nor this hand that holds the pen

life after life, life after life,
we circle back again

a beating heart,
an inhaled breath,

a certain birth,
an unknown death

all rise within a Mystery-
a pure and Soundless Deep,

where only Guru's Boundless Love
can rouse us from our sleep

Doves

on green lawns of summer
we sat cross-legged with the Guru
awed by His Inspired Talk

and even though
at Gatherings
He'd Rake us through a bed of
coals
to Blaze us Bright
and Stoke an amber glow

that we might Know Him Better

when He Praised me

His Words rose up in my heart
like a fellowship of doves

to lift me high above
my suffered self

that I might Coo
His Love

Fast Track

when this journey began
I leisurely sashayed
toward my Lord
in beaded sandals

distracted on my Way
perpetually delayed
by the mortal love

of soft skinned children
and a strong man's touch

but they have grown
and he is gone

and I have donned
my running shoes

to reach You

Friday Night Discourse

filling the Hall
knee to knee
we adjusted our pillows
and points of view

waiting in electric quiet
for the conch shell to sound

and the Inevitable
Explosion of Light

when He Entered the room

to Consume us

to unhinge the Cathedral
from this world's leaden chaos

and leave us weightless

to swoon away the evening

buoyed by His Baritone Voice

Guru Seva

I went into the marketplace
in search of perfect melons
to quench my Guru's human thirst

tapping on those rinds
I listened for a sweet response

an acknowledging refrain
of worthy juices

and on my tongue
I sang His Name
so grateful for this Gift
of Guru Seva

how could I live
if this body did not wake
to the vision of His Smile

embedded in my heart?

He Put His Stamp On Me

with an Indelible Ink
and Undeniable Grace

an Impression
of His Heart

that can never be erased

He Shook Us

until we
began

to see His Meaning

He Shocked us
with His Suddenness

of Tangible Touch

that Took us
to His Heart

acquitted of
our mortal crimes

of Separate

and Apart

High Fashion

like the emperor's new clothes
you cannot see
my true regalia

His Embrace
cloaks me
in Indivisible Finery

His Radiance
accessorizes my skin
with Wild Country Hints of Him

His Very State
Styles me
in Love's Haute Couture

His Driftwood Words

when a monsoon of sorrow
flooded every periphery of me

I floated downstream slowly

clinging only
to His Driftwood Words

His Broken Branch Dharma
Buoyed me,

drenched and bedraggled
spent with loss

His Sacred Syllables Lifted me
onto Benevolent Banks,

dried my shivered skin

and delivered me to Him

His Hands

A Current of Bliss
flows through Those Fingers

an Avalanche of Love
will send you off the slopes
and sliding

towards a very dangerous cliff

a precipice off which

you

will not be seen again

His Investment

I must confess
I was a flight risk

a high stakes gamble

but still
He Poured Every Ounce of
Himself
into my thimble

He Read me
like a trashy novel

and with One Quick Stroke
of Infinite Compassion

Edited me out

Entirely

His Mainland

in that moment on the sand
when your head is pressed
beneath His Feet

in an asana of absolute surrender
and perpetual retreat

when all your struggles
have ebbed offshore
to a distant archipelago

drop anchor Here
find your Depth

and never drift again

I Cling To You

like a tick to its dog
or moss on a rock

I cling to You

the Source

white knuckled and grasping
urgently clasping

the Tail of the Horse

I Stopped Pretending

I can't pretend
my picket fence fiction
was not distracting

but that did not prevent
the rot from setting in
or stop the paint from chipping
or keep my lover's grin
from vanishing

like You Always Told us

we wither
what is fresh today
will soon decay

it all goes
Witness this

in the final cosmic blend

only Love Persists

If Only

we didn't deny
or expect,
we wouldn't withhold
or protect,

we could
revel in

the Heart's Beginning

we could
marvel at

Your Open Eyes

Your Undisguised
 Beauty,

Your Gifts
that lift us
out of ourselves

like snakeskin
shed on a knoll,

Your Gifts
that make us
whole

Leela

once at the Ashram
when I was a young woman

my longing to see Him
became so profound

that I lost control
and abandoned myself
and everything that kept me
from Him
littered on the lawn

I ran down the rock path
to His House
uninvited

and brazenly entered
His Radiant Room

whereupon
my Lord Only Laughed
and Shouted

What took you so long?

Love Doctor

He Makes His Daily Rounds
among us

a Tireless Physician
With a Deeply Tender Touch
and a Rare Prescription

a Heart Surgeon
to suture our mortal suffering

His Procedure is Sudden

if you are willing to Receive
and Feel

if you are ready
to be healed

by the Real

Master's Plan

when by Grace

you have tiptoed
through His Open Door

been peeled back farther
than this birth to before

when life as you've known it
is shredded on the floor

exposed to the Truth
of your utter mummer's core

you are ready to
Accept Him

you are willing
to be Fashioned

by an Adept Master Craftsman

Architecturally Designed

to serve

Meditation

at first blink of morning

before thinking begins
before body resumes

and mind assumes a self

careen with Him
through Unseen Space

a Vast Unbridled Plain
where all are Free to roam

and every heart is welcomed

Home

My Balance Due

in this craving world
it doesn't matter
how much worth
I might ever accrue

I can never repay this debt

of Uncaused Joy
of Rested Heart
of Glistened Life

I owe to You

this debt
that will not let me forget

what
breath by breath
I have yet

to do
for You

My Landlord Has Evicted Me

I have gone into foreclosure,
fallen behind in my payments-
so He Himself has taken Residence
here

O how I have tried
to maintain the status quo
the unrippled flow,
scrimping, scraping by
to make the mortgage of self

but His Rhythmic Knock
was Persistent at my door,
That Repetitive Thunder
in my ear
Demanding to Enter,
Shouting at me
to Open Up!

until He Burst In,
 Face Flushed,
Waving His Eviction Notice
Wildly,
Installing Himself in every room,
Escorting me
out of everything

I ever presumed

O Blessed Am I Today

for I turned chapattis for
the Guru's feast
and spiced His chai tea
with cardamom pods

for I wiped His cook's cutting
board clean
and washed her pots
to make ready for His chutney

Blessed am I today
for I rolled out His puris
and with my own hands
lay them on the tray

Grace falls
on all who give their lives

to serve the Way

Out of Dorothy's Womb

from a Formless Place of Bright Quiet
Our Beloved was drawn here
to Quell the trembled hearts
who called for Him

with Wide Compassion
Our Beloved Appeared Here
to Guide His devotees
through the fiery course
that Realizes Him

Standing Firm
in Fijian bedrock
our Statue of Liberty
Waves His Torch for you

Pattern Maker

The Divine Tailor
spreads your bolt of self
across His cutting table

and with an Expert Eye
Sketches His Own Pattern

Stretching your yardage
far beyond its mortal width

Trimming your shredded edges
and selfish excesses

Tying up your loose ends

Hand Stitching His Own Name

into your seem

Prasad

make every mortal moment
a cup-
like upturned palms,

a vessel of reception
for Guru's Blessing Alms

Ringing Him In

I am so much more
than my appearance here

far grander than
this seeming world

I am so much less
than these bones and flesh

I am infinitely small
a speck

my poems are scrawled
on faded papyrus
painted on ancient cave walls
etched in ocean sand

they vanish
with the evening tide

rewritten outside time

eternally

to Chime Him

Safety Net

when all your lovers
have deserted you

when one by one
they have faded into moonlight
withered on the vine
left you bereft

only then
can you see
Love itself Beckoning

only then
will you hear Him
Humming your name

and in That Moment
you will be awed
by His Gesture

that Reached across eternity
to break your fall

to catch you and you and you
in His Constant Embrace

of all

Salesman

before I knew
Who
You Were

You Wooed me
with a Laughter
so Full of Poignant Life
and Boisterous Loving

You Cajoled me
with High Dharma and Discourse
that Spoke of a Bright Reality
beyond seeking

You Romanced me
with Poetic Recitations of Truth

until Your Work Took Hold

and I was sold

Sat Guru Darshan

my feet can barely touch the
ground
my heart has surely burst
for today I saw my Love,
my Lord

in bliss I am immersed

I wept to see His Stately Stride
the Lion's Royal Lope

A King Whose Glance
can Lift the veil of self
and Offer Hope

to all who seek to know the Truth
of that in which we dwell

a Silent Heart
that Sings It's Love

such things no words can tell

Spark

trust me
I have fallen down
Grief's Ravine

a vast crevasse
of suffered loss
and letting go

but all the while
He Hovered Over me
Held me Close to Him

He Tucked me in

and Woke me up

He Rappelled down
with Rope and Spark

He Lifted and Kindled me

out of the dark

The Kiss

there on the mat
waiting for His Return
from the library,
my Beloved Guru's Sandals lay

alone in that room
I smoothed the towel on His Chair
and could not help myself
but to steal upon those Thongs
and press my lips
to the soles that carry Him

how I swooned with bliss
from that stolen kiss

forgive me!

This Game Is Fixed

no matter
how you roll the dice
and try to be consoled

life
is a losing bet

whichever way
you slice it

death is what
you get

maybe now
maybe later

this churning
Russian Roulette

inevitably

death is what you always get

only Turning to Him

in this moment
this instant

transforms the lament

of the seeming body mind's

predicament

Trellised Arch

when you approach Him
with your Asiatic lilies

clasping your life of illusion
in a small bouquet

and lay it at His Feet
weeping with the Profundity
of His Blessing Regard

listen
as the gate creaks open
in His front yard

look
for a Gesture
Waving you through
His Trellised Arch

where
for God's Sake

He will surely
Shudder you Awake

Undressing at Infinity

Let's fling off our faces
and unfurl our skin
this archaic concept
of being within

that batters and bargains
for cravings fulfilled,
but does not accomplish
a moment of Still

let's take up a practice
of Lyrical Breath
that whispers of Victory
conquering death

where Guru descends
in a Formal Ordeal
and Graces our eyes
to Reveal what is Real

When Love Moved In

it was as if
His Words,

with their rounded vowels
rolling off His Royal Tongue

had oiled the rusty hinges
of my heart,

as if
the dusty shutters of my soul
now thrown open

had never known Light before

how fresh air streamed through

and His Effortless Calm

became my Bath and Balm,

when Love moved in

Without Mouthing a Word

without scalpel

or knife

He has Made an Incision

without shovel

or hoe

He Has Planted a Seed

without flint or flame

He Has Kindled a Fire

without Mouthing a Word

by Unspeakable Grace

the Guru is Heard

White Flag

Like a troop of mercenaries
You have invaded my parts;
scavenging among the blood
and breast of me,
You discovered this heart

Oh Selfish Man,
how many hearts
have You robbed and stored
to do Your Deeds?

How many homeless hearts
have You housed
with Your Rare Compassion?

That this adoration
of the Great One
may be proclaimed,
to such ends
You are sacrificed

There!

It is done.
a white flag
is woven on the wind

and my surrender is begun

Your Armory

my poems are Loaded Pistols
of Your Love

but Only You
Can Choose Your Targets
and Take Aim

Only You
Can Pull Truth's Trigger

Seriously Wounding
an unidentified number,
I too am a victim

whose chances of recovery

are slim

Anchored In His Deep

I'm Done
He Did me in
with Loving

His Words
His Silence
His Samadhi

set my fractured heart free
to swoon
Whole
in this Profundity

to notice
apparent phenomena fly by
like careening crows
in an orange sky

all the while

Anchored in His Deep

A Leaf, A Flower, A Fruit

a branch
of honeysuckle

a mala
of scented marigolds

a dahlia
of pastel persuasion

a mango an apple a pear

offered at His Feet

to celebrate

this Bright Occasion

of Universal Sacrifice

breath
 by
 breath

until

death

As If I'd Swallowed Fireflies

my blood glows luminescent
with His Shattered Light

He Inhabits
this interior

my inhaled breaths
Circumambulate
His Presence

I don't care
to keep silent about it

either

Come, Friend

stand with me
under His Waterfall

let Love's Cascade
wash us of illusion

let His Rushing Downpour
cleanse us of confusion

of wanting

and sorrow

and clinging

so that in

Pure Silence

we may hear

the Heart

Singing

Dancing Down the Light

if you see me
swaying on the sidewalk
I must have heard a wind chime
or a rustling of leaves

at the market
I can barely refrain from salsa
as coins clatter on the counter

don't get caught
in an elevator with me
if Stevie Wonder is singing a song

not only will I sing along
I am not the body
who keeps its own accord

I am subject to The Lord

and He Always Crashes Down

to Motown

Death Made Me a Yogi

I believed
in this tawdry drama
despite Your Warning

until You Showed me
the Tide of Ebb and Flow

lover bride wife widow

the fragile comings
and letting goings
of mortal love

that always finally fades
away

I had to learn the hard way

only That which is Eternal

beyond waking dreaming and
sleeping

beyond birth and death

Stays

Even Before

I saw

His Brilliant Arising

I felt His Tacit Touch

borne on a velvet Breeze
across my cheek

a Shiver of sudden laughter

an uncaused Fullness
welling in my chest

a silent dwelling in Awe

even before
I'd known

I was one of His Own

Flooded

for eons
I only skimmed my toes
on the surface of His Waters

hesitant
to Be Drenched
in His Depths

afraid to let go

to Flow

until the Pipes Burst

and Immersed Me

From the Dark

of morning puja

to the fading dim
of evening prayer

my days are filled with Him

from the stringing
of pale orchids
to the sweeping
of stone paths

my days are filled with Him

with a heart
once wrecked by sorrow

that He Salvaged
for His Own

my days are filled with Him

and Him Alone

Fully Prostrated

at His Feet
limbs extended
undefended
flat upon the floor

but how my heart
does soar!

Gold Rush

The Lord Goes Mining
in the dark interior
of self

Wielding Truth's Rock Hammer

Determined
To Strike the core

to Tap Love's Vein

He Works

with Ardent Dedication

Prospecting
to crumble

separation

He Is Calling All

so Tenderly
to Lean
into His Light

not to loiter
at the crossroads

but be Guided
by the Bright

He is Calling all

So Fiercely

to the Threshold
of His Door

where everything
is Smithereened

in the Heart's
Deep Core

He Is The Water

**He Washes
this seeming world**

**with each receding tide
and morning dew**

His Torrent of Love

makes every moment

New

He Stands in the Breakers

Wading for you

He Left the Porch Light On

so that you would not stumble
on His Flagstone Path

so that you would not fumble
for the Key

that you might clearly see

the Way
 to unlock his Door

and Enter

into Profundity

He Prioritized My Agenda

to a Single Simplicity

this worship of Real God
this habit of surrender

this abiding in
Eternal Shining

merely witnessing
searchlessly beholding

His Divine Unfolding

right now

He Scattered Neon Breadcrumbs

in this mortal forest

so that we might follow
His Bright Path
beyond self

He Tied Iridescent Ribbons
on this patterned canopy

so that we
might look
above our heads

and grow

to Notice Him

His Demonstration of Truth

I sat in the Guru's Company
studying His Demeanor

every Visible Inch
of His Bodily Human Form

observing each Expression
of Illumined Ecstasy

Displayed upon
His Face

contemplating every Rapture
of Unspoken Bliss

elevating His Eyebrows
and parting His Lips

nothing left hidden

in His Demonstration of Truth

nothing left unsaid

He Stands Forever Present
to Disarm the guarded heart

and Revive the seeming dead

His Radiance

Spreads

from the Tips of His Fingers

to the Soles of His Feet

from the Arch of His Eyebrows

to His Soft Rounded Cheek

from a Heart Loudly Beating
Out a Far Reaching Plea

Calling all

to Eternally

Love

and Be Free

His Sangha

O I have seen them
the broken hearted
lovers
who have found Him

teary eyed
loitering outside
the Temple
after morning puja

fumbling back
into daily life

carrying the Constant Thrill
of Him

embedded in their chests

His Shock of Beauty

stuns me
at the altar

where the temple Murti sits

He Extends His Hand
in Blessing

while His Lips
Purse Tight
with Samadhi

while His Heart
Spills Out

A Fount

of Love's Generosity

His Single Conversation

from the night He Sat
on Melrose Avenue

and addressed
a motley crew
of lucky aspirants
who had stumbled
into His Room

drawn like moths
to Love's Flame

Uttering the Truth

Showering this realm
with His Whisper
of Bliss Fullness

and His Ecstatic Shout-

to Now

where He Sits
at The Brightness

Reciting His Secrets
to the Earth Itself

this Avataric Revelation
of Understanding

is what His Conversation

has Always Been About

I Am Not the Body

but
as long
as I have knees

I will bend them in worship

as long
as I have hands

I will raise them
in surrender

as long
as I have eyes

I will gaze
on His Murti Form

as long
as I have a voice

I will chant His Praises

longer
than this body lives

I am His

I Didn't Get the Joke

I'd finished food preparation
in the Ashram kitchen
minutes before the lunch bell
would chime
and sat outside on the front steps
steeping in sunshine

when I saw my friend
pruning a grape arbor nearby
I walked over to chat
and casually said that
I was on a break

out of nowhere

the Guru's Voice Bellowed Down
from a balcony above me

There Are No Breaks Around
Here!

His Luxurious Laughter
Rolled over me

but could not penetrate
my shock of self-contraction
at the core

I didn't get the Joke

I could not see His Divine Humor

His Blatant Metaphor
for my benefit

I'd missed His Meaning then

There is no break in
Consciousness!

this Bliss Persists
Moment to Moment

in the Midst of all
experience

I finally get the punch line, Lord

I Have Made a Home

for myself
in the shadow of Your Ashram

where conches proclaim Your
Presence

where Japanese Maples
bow in ardor

as You Saturate the Grounds
Above Descending Down

and every day
I sweep Your Porch

with untold pleasure

I Have Worn A Suit of Armor

to protect me from
this world

I have barred
my doors and windows
and let creeping ivy
crawl

until I mouthed His Name

and the Locksmith Came

with His Round Keychain

Who set me free

to breathe

Unencumbered

I Took A Stand And Sat Down With Him

first
He Lassoed me
with an Irresistible Love

then
He Showed me
the patterns I inhabit

He Frustrated my desires
and Placed Demands on me

He Asked me
to Understand

and by some
illumined fate of mine
a Miracle Dispensed
by the Divine

my body bent
my knees bowed
I took a stand
and sat down with Him

I am sitting with Him
still

I Turn To Him

I found out
that life is lethal

bound for burial
and decay

loss and dismay

no bargaining for favors
no jargon of negotiation
to delay

the inevitable

falling away
of body parts
agendas and dreams

all of this seeming reality
becoming sepia toned
too faded to hold on to

but I still want to

so I turn to Him

I Vow To Not Forget

**His Legacy of Shimmered Light
His Incandescent Glow
not separate from Reality
what mind can never know**

**His Opulent Expression
His Brilliant Silhouette
His Unrelenting Radiance
I vow to not forget**

Invoking Him

this world crumbles
into pumice and ash

like Pompeii

when your tongue
touches the roof of your mouth
to pronounce His Name

the destruction of
self's ancient city
is Inevitable

when the Syllable of Him
rises out of your throat
like molten lava

an eruption of Bhava
will rain down
to cloak your ruins

when The Master is Invoked

Just Us

what if
there was

no me
or no you?

what on earth

would
we
do?

no longer bound
by the lonesome sound

of mine and yours-

no more of this
egoic fuss

we'd be an
Us!

let's all spin free
of I and he
and she
and me

Breathing in the Mystery!

Like Coastal Fog

everything
dissipates in the end

don't depend

on fickle weather

always turn to face

the Steady Bask

of His Midnight Sun

Like the Winter Snow

**that covers my flower garden
in a white down comforter**

**Your Blessing Grace
Settles on me**

**blanketing my heart
with an Unprecedented
Accumulation**

of Love's Precipitation

Love Is A Gateway Drug

it leads to likely incidents
of habitual dependence
on the Divine

it seduces self
to what is Greater

it reduces self
to its Common
Denominator

Prior Unity

Love is a Gateway Drug

Inhale Deeply

Love's Pigment

You

are the Primary Color
on my heart's palette

my bristle brush
dips humbly

into
Your Avataric Orange

to paint
with strokes
of Finest Detail

swirl upon swirl

a Mural of Remembrance

Forever Drenched
in Love's Pigment

that this world
will not forget

Your Parama Sapta Na

Silhouette

Master Gardener

on His way home
from the Laughing Man Library

the Guru Sat Down on the steps
of Here I Am
where a Darshan mat
had been set out

we gathered around Him
in raptured silence

as He Surrounded us
with His Extraordinary Calm

when He Stood to Leave
I could not move a muscle

as if a stake had been
driven down my spine

Pressing me deep
into His Holy Ground

Planting His Seed

O Beloved
if these days
my garden seems well tended

the Perfume of my Bloom
belongs to You!

May Your Morning

brim potent
with birdsong and prayer

in praise of the Great One

may your day
glow iridescent
with remembrance
of Him

may your evening
spill dusky

with His Sultry Calm

where peace
Congeals

in silence

Melting Clock

tick tock tick
klik klak click

time is going

are you growing?

is it showing?

are you

Shining

yet?

Morning Puja

in the early dim

after the recitation of Dharma
has been done
and a rudrashka mala
has been hung
around His Neck

after the shawl is smoothed in
place
and holy ash is pressed
against His Murti Form
with gentle strokes of Invocation

the pujarist pours
the Water from His Foot Bath
into our grateful palms

a Reservoir of Blessings
parceled out each day
with a porcelain spoon

My Heart Has Teetered

on scales

of great sorrow
and Divine Grace

vacillating
between
body mind's tragic story

and Guru's Undying
Avataric Glory

until
with Infinite Mercy

He Tipped the scale

In His Favor

My Mt. Rainer

on the eve of my son's birth
the Guru sent a message

to Offer Up a name

the child could be called Nestle
offspring of His bhakti Wesley

when asked if He Meant it
for a boy or girl

He Replied
it didn't matter

they come with or without nuts!

then Blessed us with

Tacoma

sacred mountain

rooted to earth

yet always touching sky

My Silk Defense of Self

I had intentions to impress
when I entered His House
for a Gathering

I had ransacked racks
before the long black dress
surfaced
to satisfy my sense
of style

but the second
I stepped through His Threshold
He Took One Look
and Guillotined the dress!

stunned and standing nude
before a multitude

I was unpeeled
of my flimsy sense of separation

as my silk defense of self
 cascaded to the floor

exposed to my very core

unveiled
exploded into Deeper Knowing

in the raw

Narcissus Is a Petty Thief

do not rob
your true identity
of its Fullness

by presuming
a private life

a cameo appearance
cluttered with glamorous
possibility

by assuming a separate self
clamoring to fit
into a category

when in Truth
you are Indefinable

when by Grace

you are Living Testament

you represent

Guru's Divine Accomplishment

Nothing Else Will Do

but You

no consolation of the senses
can distract attention

from my Ishta

no savored taste
or tender touch
can make me waver
in devotion

while this world continues
every sinew of me
is learning to float free

in Your Ocean

of Calm Waters

Oasis

I misunderstood
who I was
when I arrived

I assumed
I was this body mind
and tried to find
my way among the many

   until

   You

   Walked Into the Room

   and everything dissolved

   in the Heart's Refuge

Pacing For a Bloom

He is the Companion
Who Will Never Abandon you

Who is Standing
on the outskirts of self

beyond the mind's perimeter
farther than the border
of bodily desire

Waiting Waiting
in His Fullness
for the signs of

a fertile seed's Infilling

an Expectant Gardener
Pacing for a Bloom

for the Fragrance
of Understanding

that Saturates

and Transcends

the subject
of the room

Recognizing His Face

let Love
Pilfer
through

every inch
of seeming you

absconding
with all
that keeps
you

from

Recognizing

His Face

and Responding to

the Grace

of This Eternal Bond

Shambles

when His Hurricane

Hits

there is
inevitable
Upheaval

and yet
rising from the rubble

in a Shambles of surrender

He is There

to Tenderly

Caress you

He is There

to Resurrect

you

Tapas

raging through
your old growth
forest of self

He Scorches Bright
to cleanse the clench
that keeps you
from Him

that ill advised
illusion
of
I

not yet Plied Open

by His Molten Light

The Blissful Intake

of this very breath
and every breath
that follows

The Tacit Grace
of filling your lungs

to Receive Him
like a lover

Deep inside your body
Thrilled by His Beauty

until this passes
and only your grey ashes remain
to catch a salty draft
and drift away to sea

the coda
of a life lived
Fraught with
Deeper Meaning

and Tender Reverie

The Breath of Him

**O my heart has risen
weightless
like a Phoenix
swept up from ashes**

**to catch
a Draft of Him**

**He Who Carries us
Gust by Gust**

**as if we were
hot air balloons**

**filled
With the Breath of Him**

and Soaring

The Dividend

Drawn Down by an Urge
to the West of this world

The Expected One Emerged

to Wrestle back
the Integrity of Spirit

to Invest Himself in devotees
A Wordless Wealth

that we might reap
the Dividend
of what Transcends

and Mends

our mortal hearts

The Mission

it was Enough
that You Appeared

it was Sufficient
that You Submitted to Teach
every ragged pilgrim
who knocked at Your Ashram
door

it was Imperative
that You Engraved Yourself
on every heart that holds You
in Highest Esteem

it is Essential

now

that we wave our tatters of
surrender
boldly without vanity

that we broadcast Your Great
Matter

to a hungry humanity

Treading His Waters

let your body
be Engulfed
in His Velvet Lake

let your mind
Float Merry and Care Free
down His Placid Stream

let your heart
Dangle Deep
as you Undulate

and contemplate
the Great

Until I Submitted

my life was carved out
like a harvest pumpkin
gutted and pitted

until I submitted

to surrender
to my own

Conclusion

until

I allowed His Infusion

to permeate me
crown to toe

with His Inherent
Glow

We Are His Vessels

over craggy mountains
across grassy plains

He Comes for you
Reciting your name

through dense jungle

amid city din

He will Find
the very core of you

to Pour
His Loving in

we are sturdy porcelain

Vessels of Him

When My Pen Refused To Write

construction had been completed
on Plain Talk Chapel
and Beloved was Gracing us
with an Inaugural Discourse

I ran with notebook in hand
to sit in the first row
directly in front of Him

determined to capture
every pearl on paper

but just as He
Began to Speak
the pen refused to write
despite me

in that moment
the Guru Looked at me
and Murmured Wordlessly

Put your pen down
Put your pad away
Listen to Me now
Receive Me deeper

and so I did
I straightened my asana
and Invoked Him

and just like that
He Unzipped my chest
and with the Bellows of His Breath
Filled me with His Excess

You Have Sung the Sacred Songs

my Lord
since our first encounter,
but these ears have been bound
by a lonely heartbeat

You Have Sung the Sacred Songs,
my Lord
with An Open Throated Candor,
but these breasts have been bound
by their manly caress

You Have Sung the Sacred Songs,
my Lord
since Your Perfect Sacrifice
Demanded it,
but this mind has been bound
by a secular profundity

You Have Sung the Sacred Songs,
my Lord
since Our God Burst Through
You
Raving in a passion for Truth!

Master, O Master!

these ears have heard the night
quiet
these breasts have felt a heart
behind them
this mind has worn weary
of its knowing

You Have Sung the Sacred Songs, my Lord

now may I offer a refrain

Index of Poems by Page

All Along pg. 1
Almost Erased pg. 2
Archer pg. 3
Arias of Ecstasy pg. 4
Arrival Mala pg. 5
At Your Altar pg. 6
Boutonniere pg. 7
Branded By Your Love pg. 8
Chameleon pg. 9
Circle Dance pg. 11
Clairol pg. 12
Deluge pg. 14
Despite My Grasp pg. 15
A Soundless Deep pg. 16
Doves pg. 17
Fast Track pg. 18
Friday Night Discourse pg. 19
Guru Seva pg. 20
He Put His Stamp On Me pg. 21
He Shook Us pg. 22
High Fashion pg. 23
His Driftwood Words pg. 24
His Hands pg. 25
His Investment pg. 26
His Mainland pg. 27
I Cling To You pg. 28
I Stopped Pretending pg. 29
If Only pg. 30
Leela pg. 31
Love Doctor pg. 32
Master's Plan pg. 33
Meditation pg. 34
My Balance Due pg. 35
My Landlord Has Evicted Me pg. 36

O Blessed Am I Today pg. 37
Out of Dorothy's Womb pg. 38
Pattern Maker pg. 39
Prasad pg. 40
Ringing Him In pg. 41
Safety Net pg. 42
Salesman pg. 43
Sat Guru Darshan pg. 44
Spark pg. 45
The Kiss pg. 46
This Game Is Fixed pg. 47
Trellised Arch pg. 48
Undressing At Infinity pg. 49
When Love Moved In pg. 50
Without Mouthing A Word pg. 51
White Flag pg. 52
Your Armory pg. 53
Anchored In His Deep pg. 54
A Leaf, A Flower, A Fruit pg. 55
As If I'd Swallowed Fireflies pg. 56
Come, Friend pg. 57
Dancing Down the Light pg. 58
Death Made Me A Yogi pg. 59
Even Before pg. 60
Flooded pg. 61
From the Dark pg. 62
Fully Prostrated pg. 63
Gold Rush pg. 64
He Is Calling All pg. 65
He Is the Water pg. 66
He Left the Porch Light On pg. 67
He Prioritized My Agenda pg. 68
He Scattered Neon Breadcrumbs pg. 69
His Demonstration of Truth pg. 70

His Radiance pg. 71
His Sangha pg. 72
His Shock of Beauty pg. 73
His Single Conversation pg. 74
I Am Not the Body pg. 75
I Didn't Get the Joke pg. 76
I Have Made a Home pg. 78
I Have Worn A Suit of Armor pg. 79
I Took A Stand and Sat Down With Him pg. 80
I Turn to Him pg. 81
I Vow To Not Forget pg. 82
Invoking Him pg. 83
Just Us pg. 84
Like Coastal Fog pg. 85
Like the Winter Snow pg. 86
Love Is a Gateway Drug pg. 87
Love's Pigment pg. 88
Master Gardener pg. 89
May Your Morning pg. 90
Melting Clock pg. 91
Morning Puja pg. 92
My Heart Has Teetered pg. 93
My Mt. Rainer pg. 94
My Silk Defense of Self pg. 95
Narcissus Is a Petty Thief pg. 96
Nothing Else Will Do pg. 97
Oasis pg. 98
Pacing For a Bloom pg. 99
Recognizing His Face pg. 100
Shambles pg. 101
Tapas pg. 102
The Blissful Intake pg. 103
The Breath of Him pg. 104
The Dividend pg. 105
The Mission pg. 106
Treading In His Waters pg. 107

Until I Submitted pg. 108
We Are His Vessels pg. 109
When My Pen Refused To Write pg. 110
You Have Sung the Sacred Songs, My Lord pg. 111

To find out more about Avatar Adi Da Samraj and His Reality-Way

Visit the ADIDAM website: www.adidam.org

Made in the USA
San Bernardino, CA
01 July 2014